Info Tech Careers

Stuart A. Kallen

ReferencePoint Press®

San Diego, CA

About the Author

Stuart A. Kallen is the author of more than 350 nonfiction books for children and young adults. He has written on topics ranging from the theory of relativity to the art of electronic dance music. In addition Kallen has written award-winning children's videos and television scripts. In his spare time he is a singer, songwriter, and guitarist in San Diego.

For more information, contact:
ReferencePoint Press, Inc.
PO Box 27779
San Diego, CA 92198
www.ReferencePointPress.com

Picture Credits:

Cover: SeventyFour
  6: Maury Aaseng
13: Monkey Business Images/Shutterstock.com
20: wavebreakmedia/Shutterstock.com
60: Gorodenkoff/Shutterstock.com

LIBRARY OF CONGRESS CATALOGING-IN-PUBLICATION DATA

Name: Kallen, Stuart A., 1955– author.
Title: Info Tech Careers/by Stuart A. Kallen.
Description: San Diego, CA: ReferencePoint Press, Inc., 2019. | Series: STEM Careers series | Includes bibliographical references and index. | Audience: Grades 9-12.
Identifiers: LCCN 2018005905 (print) | LCCN 2018008236 (ebook) | ISBN 9781682824368 (eBook) | ISBN 9781682824351 (hardback)
Subjects: LCSH: Information technology—Vocational guidance—Juvenile literature.
Classification: LCC T58.5 (ebook) | LCC T58.5 .K338 2019 (print) | DDC 004.023—dc23
LC record available at https://lccn.loc.gov/2018005905

Contents

Good Prospects, Great Pay

In 2016 the tech industry accounted for 8 percent of all economic activity in the United States, generating more than $1.3 trillion. Around one in twenty Americans worked in the tech industry. And the number of jobs involving web development, database administration, information security, and other information technology (IT) jobs increased by 3 percent in 2016 alone. As tech researcher Tim Herbert states on technology trade association CompTIA's website: "Tech sector employment outpaces other notable segments of the economy, including construction, finance and insurance, transportation and warehousing, and arts, entertainment, and recreation."

Despite the growth of IT jobs, there has long been a shortage of IT workers, as IBM vice president of talent Joanna Daly told the Associated Press in 2017: "There's a half-million open technology jobs in this country and we're only producing 50,000 computer science graduates each year. So for the industry, we have a technology skills gap."

With the tech industry facing a chronic shortage of IT workers, those individuals with information technology skills rarely worry about finding employment. The unemployment rate among database administrators was around 1 percent in 2017 while computer network architects faced only a 0.6 percent rate of unemployment. This compares to a 4.7 percent rate for all workers. Low unemployment rates translate into high wages. The median pay for a computer and information technology worker in 2017 was $83,000, more than two times the $37,000 average for all jobs.

Opportunities for those with IT expertise extend to industries not traditionally associated with tech—nearly every company needs a cutting-edge digital platform to survive. These enterprises are look-

4

ing for workers who fall into a new category known as "hybrid technical roles"—that is, they possess both technology skills and business expertise. In 2016 there were over 250,000 hybrid technical job openings. As software developer Neel Somani states on the Rasmussen College website: "A large part of the reason why technical skills are becoming increasingly common in business positions is because of the growth of data science. With the massive amount of data available to businesses today, it's crucial that decision-makers have the skills necessary to analyze this information." Those who possess this new skill set can earn comparably high starting salaries while seizing opportunities for future career growth.

Apprentice Programs

Tech companies are ubiquitous at college career fairs. These employers are not necessarily looking for people who have majored in IT fields, however. They are interested in candidates who can be trained for specific IT jobs. And tech companies from small start-ups to major corporations are investing in apprenticeship programs that offer a mix of classroom and paid on-the-job training.

Apprentice programs are costly for corporations; the average tech company spends about $54,000, including salary, for each apprentice in programs that typically last one year. But what is costly for a company is beneficial to a student seeking to move into an IT career. Apprentices earn a living, gain lifelong skills, and avoid spending tens of thousands of dollars in pursuit of advanced degrees in college. Along the way, they take on new challenges, learn to solve novel problems, and push their creativity to the limit while moving up a few income brackets.

Coding and Communicating

Technology companies are looking for developers, computer programmers, systems analysts, information security analysts, IT managers, and those who can provide general technical support. This means jobs are available to those with many interests and capabilities. But students aiming for careers in IT are required to possess

Info Tech Careers

Occupation	Minimum Education Requirements	2016 Median Pay
Computer and information research scientist	Master's degree	$111,840
Computer and information systems manager	Bachelor's degree	$135,800
Computer hardware engineer	Bachelor's degree	$115,080
Computer network architect	Bachelor's degree	$101,210
Computer support specialist	Associate's degree	$52,160
Computer systems analyst	Bachelor's degree	$87,220
Database administrator	Bachelor's degree	$84,950
Electrical and electronics engineer	Bachelor's degree	$96,270
Information security analyst	Bachelor's degree	$92,600
Software developer	Bachelor's degree	$102,280
Web developer	Associate's degree	$66,130

Source: US Department of Labor, *Occupational Outlook Handbook*, 2017. www.bls.gov.

a few fundamental skills to satisfy employers. Every IT professional needs to be able to write computer code in several different programming languages, including HTML and C++. Successful coders are logical thinkers and problem solvers who have a strong overall understanding of different technologies and information systems.

Good communication skills are another necessity for survival in the IT world. While the stereotype of an IT professional is an introvert who works long hours wearing earphones and coding into the night, this is not the workplace reality. Successful IT workers are team players who enhance collaboration among their colleagues. They are called upon to translate technical concepts into plain English for multiple stakeholders in a project that might include business executives, sales and marketing associates, and others who are not technically inclined.

Networking is an extension of good communication, as career consultant Alison Doyle explains on the Balance website: "[Networking] requires gathering groups of people in a working environment to share what they know, in order to build a system of knowledge within an organization that is more than the sum of its parts. Knowledge networks require individual IT professionals to be open with their knowledge and to be open and curious about learning new things from their colleagues."

Ample Job Opportunities

According to the Bureau of Labor Statistics (BLS), employment for information technology professionals is expected to grow by 13 percent through 2026. This projected growth is pegged to an industry that is expanding at warp speed. Mark Smukler, cofounder of the software firm Bixby, put the BLS statistic in perspective in a 2017 *Forbes* article: "Tech isn't for everyone, but tech is probably the single greatest opportunity that exists for millennials today. There's still a large shortage of technical expertise across most [industries] and a career in tech can be one of the most rewarding jobs in many ways." The news could not be better for those who are fascinated by the digital world that is becoming more reliant on the skills of IT professionals every day.

Web Developer

What Does a Web Developer Do?

In 2017 the Internet services company Netcraft determined there were more than 1.7 billion websites online. That's more than five times the number of sites that were on the Internet in 2011. Millions of these websites are created and maintained by trained web developers. These professionals "tell" a website how to function by writing computer code using programming languages like HTML and XML.

Web developers meet with clients to discuss their website needs. Typical clients want websites that can be used for e-commerce, business promotion, news and commentary, gaming, or social media services. Web developers work with web designers to explore the types of graphics, photos, sounds, and other features that make a website attractive, functional, and secure. After a website is completed, the web developer monitors web traffic, provides feedback to clients, and periodically tests the website to ensure it is in good working order.

While some web developers handle all aspects of website creation, others are specialists. Back-end web developers specialize in

At a Glance

Web Developer

Minimum Educational Requirements
Associate's degree

Personal Qualities
Strong programming skills, good communicator, patience

Certification and Licensing
Certified Professional Web Developer

Working Conditions
Full-time work with overtime in a casual workplace environment

Salary
$66,130 median annual pay in 2016

Number of Jobs
162,900 in 2016

Future Job Outlook
15 percent growth through 2026

what is referred to as server-side scripting. This is the technical framework of a website that users never see. Back-end developers focus on the inner workings of a site using coding languages like Ruby or PHP to make sure that a website works well with servers—computers that provide data to other computers—and is optimized for speed and efficiency.

Front-end web developers build on the work of back-end developers using front-end coding languages like JavaScript, HTML5, and CSS3. Front-end developers focus on user-side scripting, providing what is sometimes referred to as the "human" aspect of a website. This aspect is what visitors to a website see, hear, touch, and experience.

Some web developers work as webmasters, who maintain websites and keep them updated. Webmasters solve technical problems, approve content created by designers and others, and ensure a website works with every type of browser, including Safari, Microsoft Edge, and Chrome.

Full-stack web developers combine front-end and back-end skills. They are knowledgeable in every aspect of web development and understand the technology behind computers, web servers, and the Internet. Full-stack developers can advise clients on web development strategy and make educated predictions about issues that may need to be addressed in the future as technology changes.

Using a car analogy, back-end developers create the chassis, motor, transmission, tires, and drivetrain of a car while front-end developers work on the body design and interior aspects like the dashboard, seats, and sound system. The webmaster can be thought of as a mechanic who does tune-ups, runs diagnoses, and ensures that the car functions in every type of environment.

Beyond mastering coding languages, software, and computer hardware, web developers need people skills to succeed with clients. As web developer Langston Taylor explains to the University of North Carolina at Chapel Hill's student newspaper, the *Daily Tar Heel*:

> You need to have a website up by a deadline. You have to figure out how to both get the technical stuff done as well as communicate with the client to figure out exactly what they

want. You have to translate [suggestions from] the client, who's not necessarily a web [developer], and their desires into something that you can do and works well for them. It's a great opportunity to work on that in the real world.

How Do You Become a Web Developer?

Education

In a room full of web developers, you will find people with associate's degrees, bachelor's degrees in computer science, master's degrees, and even a few with only a high school education. What most web developers have in common is a talent for graphic design and a keen understanding of HTML, JavaScript, and other coding languages. One of the world's most famous web developers, Facebook founder Mark Zuckerberg, taught himself to write code at age six. And many other (less famous) web developers learned to build websites on their own.

The demand for people with web development skills is so great that even those self-taught individuals can find work without attending college. Sergei Garcia is one of those self-educated web developers. He learned JavaScript on a free website called Codecademy and by reading an e-book called *Eloquent JavaScript* by Marijn Haverbeke. As Garcia explains on the website freeCodeCamp: "That book was tough—especially if you're just learning programming like I was back then. But I'm glad I didn't give up and kept at it. It was phenomenal due to the vast scope of programming concepts it covers. . . . Once you finish this book, then you can finally say with confidence that you have a good grasp [of] JavaScript." Garcia went on to teach himself web design and various other programming languages through another website called Code School, which charges users around $30 a month. After completing his self-education in 2015, Garcia found work as a front-end developer for one of *Forbes* magazine's top 500 companies.

Some individuals like Garcia find success through diligent self-education. But most employers prefer web developers who have at least an associate's degree since the job requires more than just coding. Some schools offer what is called coding boot camp, a twenty-four-week course that teaches coding, graphic design, and career development.

Those students who pursue a two-year associate's degree learn full-stack coding skills and also take courses in business communications, e-commerce strategies, graphic production, and composition. Associate's degree programs also include electives like fine arts, behavioral sciences, and natural sciences. Some students commit themselves to earning a bachelor of computer sciences degree, commonly referred to as a CS. This math-heavy program includes courses in computer programming, algorithms, data structures, logic and computation, calculus, linear algebra, and statistics, as well as electives like operating systems, real-time computing, artificial intelligence, and software testing.

Certification

Web developers do not need to be certified in order to find work, but numerous organizations offer professional certification, which can lead to greater employment opportunities and higher salaries. For example, those individuals who pass exams offered by Web-Professional.org can become certified professional webmasters, developers, and designers.

Internships

Many companies offer summer intern positions to computer science students who are still in school. Interns are typically paired with mentors and collaborate with others on group projects. Internships offer good networking opportunities and often lead to full-time employment upon graduation.

Skills and Personality

Writing computer code hour after hour every day—and relating to clients and other workers—requires technical talents and what are called soft skills or people skills. On the technical side, web developers need strong programming skills so that writing code becomes second nature. The ability to concentrate on extremely complex lines of code for long periods of time is also necessary along with an eye for detail; even the slightest error can result in a website performing poorly or crashing. An analytical mind-set is useful for problem solving, and the ability to see the big picture along with the smallest details is vital.

The old saying "Patience is a virtue" is especially true for web developers. Websites are never completed; clients often require changes and updates and quibble over the smallest details. Web developers need to remain calm and understanding during what might seem like a never-ending development process.

Good communication skills are also a must. Web developers are often required to translate technical jargon into simple terms for multiple parties who are involved in creating a website, including designers, illustrators, copywriters, and other personnel.

Garcia adds his own "secret sauce" for success. For him, it's important for web developers to love what they do since those who are passionate stand out from the crowd, be generous with knowledge because it enhances teamwork, and always be on the lookout for new things. He says, "Whether it be by reading blogs, spending lots of time in programming related discussions, or even talking about what's new in web development during lunch breaks . . . [b]eing on the lookout for new things all the time allows the best developers to always stay ahead of the curve."

On the Job

Employers

In 2016 there were around 162,900 jobs for web developers, according to the Bureau of Labor Statistics (BLS). About one in five web developers worked in the publishing industy for newspapers, magazines, and other media. Others worked in businesses that specialized in computer systems design, advertising and public relations, and scientific and technical consulting.

Around 16 percent of web developers are freelancers who work on a project-to-project basis. They usually join a team already assembled at a workplace and help create a website. As

A web developer meets with a client to discuss goals for the client's website. Some web developers handle all aspects of website creation while others become specialists in a particular phase of web development.

the name implies, freelancers have more freedom than those who punch a time clock every day. However, the self-employed often need to work harder, as freelance developer Thomas Jost told Business.com in 2018: "[A freelancer must be] willing to go above and beyond what a salaried employee would be willing to do. The predominant driving force here is word of mouth—freelancers are relying on . . . referrals to keep their lights on. Salaried employees are only worried about being productive enough to not get fired most of the time."

Working Conditions

Most web developers are full-time employees who are sometimes required to work overtime when rushing to meet project deadlines. Most workplaces have a casual atmosphere; many web developers listen to music all day on their earphones as they work. In addition to coding, web developers usually spend several hours a day communicating with clients by text and e-mail or participating in conference calls. As self-employed web developer Jules Gravinese explains on the career website Vault: "I service nearly 50 domains so there is quite a bit of support going on. I never leave anyone out of touch when they need assistance or have an issue." Gravinese tries to complete her calls and e-mails before lunch. After eating lunch at her desk, she spends the afternoon coding.

Earnings

The BLS reports that the median annual wage for web developers in 2016 was $66,130. That means that half of all professionals in this field earned more than the median while half earned less. The lowest 10 percent of web developers earned $35,380 while the most experienced, in the top 10 percent, earned more than $119,550. Freelancers generally either charge per hour or by project. According to the employment website Upwork, freelancers just starting out can earn around $15 an hour while those who have experience can earn up to $150 per hour.

Opportunities for Advancement

Web developers who pursue continuing education and training opportunities can quickly advance from entry-level positions to positions with greater responsibilities and commensurate pay. Some developers who build a strong portfolio at a small firm can move on to top companies like Apple, Google, and HP that offer premium salaries and benefits.

What Is the Future Outlook for Web Developers?

Web development is a growing field, and web developers are in great demand. According to the BLS, total employment for web developers is expected to grow by 15 percent through 2026, much faster than the 7 percent average for all occupations. This positive job outlook is explained on the website GitHub by Brandon Swift, cofounder of Santa Barbara–based Volt Commerce: "Everyone wants a website. As a web developer, you'll never be short on work. I mean never!"

Find Out More

Codecademy
49 W. Twenty-Seventh St.
New York, NY 10001
website: www.codecademy.com

This online school offers free coding lessons in numerous programming languages, including Git, AngularJS, JavaScript, and CSS. Students can sign up and begin coding within minutes.

freeCodeCamp
website: www.freecodecamp.org

This nonprofit organization offers a free interactive online learning platform, a community forum, and chat rooms for those interested in learning to code. Students work to complete assignments, and after completing all project tasks, they are partnered with nonprofits to help build web applications.

International Web Association
556 S. Fair Oaks Ave.
Pasadena, CA 91105
website: http://iwanet.org

This nonprofit professional association provides educational and certification standards for web professionals, with more than one hundred official chapters in 106 countries. The association offers courses in web technologies, programming, graphics, and web business.

WebProfessionals.org
PO Box 584
Washington, IL 61571-0584
website: https://webprofessionals.org

This organization has been providing education, certification, and community support since 1997. Prospective web developers can find online training options, networking opportunities, career counseling, and job offerings on the organization's website.

Computer Systems Administrator

What Does a Computer Systems Administrator Do?

The last Friday of every July is celebrated as Systems Administrator Appreciation Day at numerous tech companies throughout the world, including those in the United States, the United Kingdom, Japan, and Russia. Computer systems administrator Ted Kekatos created the annual event, also known as Sysadmin Day, in July 2000 to commemorate the hard work performed by those workers who spend their days managing servers, desktop computers, and mobile computer equipment. Kekatos told the *Devolutions* blog in 2017 the three reasons he became a computer systems administrator: "To work with new technology; to help and educate users; and to learn something new every day."

Sysadmins are formally called network and computer systems

administrators, and many companies would cease to function without them. Computer systems administrators manage all servers, computers, and other IT infrastructure at an organization. They are responsible for installing, organizing, and supporting the day-to-day operations of information technology infrastructure. This infrastructure includes local area networks (LANs), which are interconnected computers within a limited area like a building. Computer systems administrators also oversee wide area networks (WANs), which extend over large geographic areas, and intranets, which are private networks only accessible to those within an organization. Computer systems administrators set up e-mail servers, file servers, and other servers required by a company. They install apps and security patches, update operating systems, and perform many other tasks to ensure all necessary services are glitch-free and running properly. Computer systems administrators are also responsible for telecommunication networks that allow employees to work from home or from the road.

While the job is complicated, it can be reduced to three primary tasks: deployment, monitoring, and maintaining. Deployment involves setting up new hardware, like computers, and installing operating systems and software. Monitoring tasks include making sure hardware is working correctly. And maintaining tasks include fixing errors in the system and updating software and equipment.

Beyond working with hardware and software, computer systems administrators need to be team players. They work with network architects to design and analyze network models and help managers make decisions about hardware and software upgrades. Computer systems administrators have to ensure that employee workstations are properly functioning and fix problems for those employees who are not as technically gifted. They might also train new users on company hardware and software and provide general tech support to all employees.

Small companies generally have a single computer systems administrator who performs all tasks required of the job. Larger companies might have specialists who focus on specific roles. Those individuals who specialize as network administrators maintain the routers, switches, and other infrastructure. They monitor

LAN and WAN networks and Internet and intranet systems in order to improve performance, maintain security, and fix problems with network software and hardware.

A server administrator maintains the system of servers. These large, high-powered computers process requests and deliver data to computer users on a local area network. A sysadmin known by the online name indrapr explains the importance of maintaining servers on the *SimplerCloud* blog: "[Server administrators] ensure that Internet connection in the office is working, the mail server is running and processing emails that are sent and received by all staff within the organization. Without these basic operations, you will not be able to do anything which requires Internet connection, such as surfing the web or checking your emails."

How Do You Become a Computer Systems Administrator?

Education

Students who wish to become computer systems administrators can follow several different paths to achieve their career goals. Some sysadmins are self-taught, meaning they set up their own systems at home and learn from books, online videos, and other media sources. However, most companies require computer systems administrators to hold a bachelor's degree in computer science or information technology. Degree programs focus on fundamental concepts behind computer network and systems administration and cover operating systems such as Windows, Unix, and Linux.

Like most other tech jobs, computer systems administrators must be self-learners willing to keep up with the latest developments in their field. Most individuals in this role take continuing education courses and regularly attend systems administrator conventions. One of the most popular sysadmin conferences is known as LISA (Large Installation System Administration Conference), which includes six days of tutorial training sessions, technical conferences, and vendor displays. Sysadmin for Sun Microsystems Tim Kennedy explains the benefits of such gatherings on the information-sharing website Quora: "[Conferences] provide fantastic learning experiences, not just in the sessions, but in the breakout forums, or at dinner or in a bar, with people who do what you want to do. Just the chance to network with people in your profession makes the . . . [conference fees] worth [it]."

Certification

Certifications are important for prospective computer systems administrators. According to the magazine *PC World*, 68 percent of hiring managers in the IT industry give a "medium or high priority" to job candidates who possess certification. Students who pass exams can obtain certification in programming, servers, applications, and databases. One of the most common accreditations is the Microsoft Certified Solutions Associate (MCSA). This certification is awarded in a number of specializations, such as Windows 10, Office 365, and SQL Server. Students can prep for the test by taking courses in a number of settings, including Microsoft training locations, certified courses in high school or college, and through self-study on the company website. After obtaining an MCSA, computer systems administrators can obtain more advanced accreditation; a Microsoft Certified Systems Engineer (MCSE) certificate focuses on the Microsoft Windows NT operating system, related desktop systems, networking, and Microsoft's BackOffice server products.

Multinational technology company Cisco provides five levels of certification for computer systems administrators: Entry, Associate, Professional, Expert, and Architect. The Entry level is for individuals interested in starting a career as a network professional while the Associate level is aimed at those wanting to perform network installations and troubleshooting. Professional and Expert certifications cover issues that include routing and switching, security, and cloud computing. A Cisco Certified Architect provides the highest level of accreditation available and is awarded to those professionals who design networks for global organizations.

Internships

Most companies offer summer intern positions to computer science students who wish to learn computer systems administration.

The job of the computer systems administrator includes managing servers, computers, and other IT infrastructure. He or she is also responsible for providing support for a company's day-to-day IT operations.

Candidates work with teams in a fast-moving environment to integrate, deploy, and support complex computer systems. Interns participate in research and development, problem-solving, maintenance, and other tasks. To qualify for internships, candidates are required to be enrolled in a college or university, and they must be familiar with various operating systems, installation procedures, coding, and process management.

Skills and Personality

Computer systems administrators need strong technical abilities to thoroughly understand one or more major computer operating systems. While the Windows operating system is most commonly used throughout the world, knowledge of other systems like Linux, Android, and iOS expand employment opportunities. Strong analytical skills allow administrators to mentally model a running system, evaluate networks, and envision where problems might be occurring. Computer systems administrators need to be multitaskers since they are expected to handle numerous issues and problems at the same time.

Since computer systems administrators work in office settings, they must have good communication skills, including listening to workers who have problems and explaining solutions to those who lack strong tech training. As with most jobs, teamwork is important as Reddit sysadmin Jason Harvey explains in a Q&A on the professional networking website Spiceworks:

> I work with people who are extremely talented, respectful of each other, and dedicated to helping one another. If there is a site issue, we don't waste time assigning blame (except maybe in jest), we simply work as a team to get it fixed. . . . As a team, we make the calls on how the site should be run from a technical, community, and business perspective. There are obviously scenarios where an individual will need to take the responsibility of making a call, but even then those calls are discussed with the entire team first.

Employers

Approximately 391,300 people worked as computer systems administrators in 2016. About one in five worked for employers involved in computer systems design and related services. These companies, like IBM and Oracle, market software, IT infrastructure, and computer hardware. Beyond the tech industry, almost every business relies heavily on technology, which means job opportunities for sysadmins abound in every economic sector, including finance, health care, gaming, sports, and other entertainment.

Working Conditions

Computer systems administrators work full-time and often work overtime to ensure that networks are operating properly night and day. In a single shift, a computer systems administrator may work among stacks of servers, sort through tangles of network cables, tap on keyboards at employee workstations, and deal with minor and major digital disasters. The job can be stressful when malfunctions shut down the communications, e-mail, and other important systems workers depend on. The job is not for the faint of heart who want to spend their days undisturbed in a cubicle listening to music. Companies depend on their networks for so many tasks that when problems occur, they must be fixed quickly and completely. And the job never ends, as indrapr explains:

> Most system administrators are always on-call, since they have system and network infrastructure which needs to run 24×7. . . . A system administrator can get paged or called at 3 am . . . when a mail server goes down, or when the Internet connection suddenly stops working. But the most important thing is that they are the ones who must ensure that all servers are functioning, the network is run ning and healthy, *all the time*.

Earnings

The median pay for a computer systems administrator in 2016 was $79,700. Half of the workers in the occupation earned less while the lowest 10 percent of earners brought in $48,870. The highest 10 percent of computer systems administrators earned more than $127,610. The annual median wage was higher—above $84,000—for those computer systems administrators working in the information technology, finance, and insurance sectors. A lower median wage of $68,510 was earned by those who worked in educational services and government agencies.

Opportunities for Advancement

Entry-level employees start out with the title junior systems administrator. They assist those with more experience. After several years on the job, those in a junior position can move up to intermediate roles. Those individuals referred to as senior computer systems administrators generally have five or more years of experience. However, the job titles are fluid, and some companies do not differentiate between junior, intermediate, and senior computer systems administrators. Regardless of title, those with the most experience earn the highest salaries.

What Is the Future Outlook for Computer Systems Administrators?

Employment for computer systems administrators is expected to grow by 6 percent through 2026, almost as fast as average for all occupations. According to the Bureau of Labor Statistics, the outlook is better for those who specialize in network administration. As more firms invest in mobile networks and cloud services, job growth for network administrators is predicted to grow by 20 percent through 2026. In general, job opportunities for this profession will remain strong because, according to Kekatos, "sysadmins are part of a great big global community of professionals who . . . work very hard to make everyone else's lives easier."

Find Out More

Association for Computing Machinery (ACM)
2 Penn Plaza
New York, NY 10121
website: www.acm.org

The ACM consists of computing educators, researchers, and professionals who promote dialogue, sharing of resources, and recognition of technical excellence. The association also promotes computer science and software engineering curriculum from the middle- and high-school level to the undergraduate, graduate, and doctoral level.

Computing Research Association (CRA)

1828 L St. NW
Washington, DC 20036
website: https://cra.org

The CRA is dedicated to linking computer researchers from industry, academia, and government. The association has a strong focus on students, and its website provides information about research grants, awards programs, graduate school options, and career building.

IEEE Computer Society

2001 L St. NW
Washington, DC 20036
website: www.computer.org

The IEEE Computer Society is dedicated to computer science and technology and provides information about networking and career development for educators, engineers, IT professionals, and students. The website contains numerous educational and career-building resources, including online courses and books, webinars, scholarships, and certification prep.

USENIX Association

2560 Ninth St.
Berkeley, CA 94710
website: www.usenix.org

USENIX is also known as the Advanced Computing Systems Association. It is a community of engineers, systems administrators, scientists, and technicians that hosts advanced computing conferences, promotes research, and shares information. The student section on the website provides tech sessions and tutorials, grant opportunities, and information about student paper awards.

Database Administrator

Database Administrator

Minimum Educational Requirements
Bachelor's degree

Personal Qualities
Analytical skills, good communicator, team player, detail oriented

Certification
Microsoft, Oracle, and other database manufacturers offer certification in their systems

Working Conditions
Full-time work with occasional late-night hours in a high-pressure environment

Salary
$84,950 median annual pay in 2016

Number of Jobs
119,500 in 2016

Future Job Outlook
11 percent growth through 2026

What Does a Database Administrator Do?

Data is a short word with a simple meaning; it refers to facts and statistics related to anything. Databases are collections of data. From there things get complicated. Numerous organizations from government agencies to shopping websites, social media networks, and financial institutions maintain vast databases. These databases are filled with billions of pieces of data, including customer information like names, ages, phone numbers, addresses, bank balances, credit ratings, shopping histories, political affiliations, and more.

Some databases are specific. Bibliographic databases kept by libraries and media organizations are filled with literature, nonfiction books, government reports, newspaper and magazine articles, brochures, and various publishing files. Other databases contain data about

25

music, movies, and art. For example, IMDb, originally known as the Internet Movie Database, contains one of the most comprehensive collections of data about movies, TV shows, actors, characters, and production crews. The largest databases are managed by banking, manufacturing, health care, and insurance firms. Whatever their purpose, databases make up the basic foundation of technological society. Private company databases are used by employees and customers while public databases, such as the online encyclopedia Wikipedia, can be accessed by the general public.

Professionals who manage the countless databases on public and private servers are called database administrators (DBAs). They use software to store and organize data such as medical records, bookkeeping information, or customer shipping records. It is said that those who work as DBAs have three important jobs: protect the data, protect the data, and protect the data. This task is becoming more important with each passing year. Centralized databases are extremely attractive to hackers who can earn large sums of money selling pilfered data. Security analyst Mark Nunnikhoven told CNN in 2017: "As we do more and more of our business online, and as criminals realize the value of the data that organizations are protecting, we're seeing more big-name breaches, more high-profile breaches."

Database administrators protect against hackers by closely monitoring databases. Auditing, or tracking activity on a database, is particularly critical in discovering hacks and preventing breaches. DBAs also strictly control who can access a database by implementing secure methods of authentication and authorization. Authentication requires usernames and passwords. Authorization is a system that limits user access to various parts of a database.

Beyond protecting against hackers, DBAs also need to protect databases from other problems. DBAs are responsible for shielding data in cases of power failure, equipment breakdown, and software glitches. They take measures to back up databases in the cloud or on servers specifically designed for backup purposes. DBAs develop, implement, and test recovery plans. When failures occur, database administrators take steps to recover data and return the database to operational status as quickly as possible. However, the cost of backups can be high for large businesses, and the DBA must evaluate costs versus risk when applying backup technology.

In addition to protecting the data, a database administrator must install, configure, and upgrade database software on computers, servers, and operating systems. When new servers are installed, DBAs ensure that the data gets properly transferred from the old server. Database administrators must also devise storage and capacity plans; they need to monitor available disc space on computer hardware and watch growth trends to allow databases to be properly expanded when necessary.

Database administrators must ensure that servers are running as efficiently as possible and tune them for better performance. This task compels DBAs to identify digital bottlenecks that can slow down data processing speeds. To fix problems, database software might need to be reconfigured to increase speed and capacity.

Most DBAs perform general duties, but some are specialists. Systems DBAs work with the physical and technical aspects of a database, installing security upgrades and patches to prevent bugs. They focus on system architecture to make sure that computers, servers, and other database hardware are functioning properly. Those who work as application DBAs focus on specific applications rather than overall database systems. They write code to create database software designed for a specific purpose, such as customer service.

How Do You Become a Database Administrator?

Education

Most database administrators have a bachelor's degree in computer science, information technology, or other related subject. Students who wish to work as a DBA focus on several subjects, including database theory, database design, and operating systems like Windows and Linux. Students learn the database language Structured Query Language (SQL) and work with database management software like Microsoft SQL Server. They study storage technologies and networking, and they learn about database maintenance, recovery, and security. Major firms with large databases might require workers to hold a master's degree in data management or database management.

Successful DBAs are lifelong self-learners who continue to expand their expertise after landing a job. As information technology professor Kevin Hawkins explains on the Cyber Security website: "The best thing to do is . . . to continually train yourself by taking classes that are offered, working for a decent company that offers you continuing technology classes to keep you on top of your field, and take any kind of classes that are available on your own. . . . Buy a book, take some certification courses . . . that pertain to your field."

Certification and Licensing

There are numerous certifications available for database administrators that will help them secure jobs, advance their careers, and earn higher salaries. Most are offered by vendors like IBM, Oracle, and Microsoft. The IBM Professional Certification Program provides candidates the opportunity to earn credentials that verify their proficiency in database management. The IBM Certified Database Administrator for Linux, UNIX, and Windows offers three levels of certification.

Oracle University, hosted by the database technology company Oracle Corporation, offers training and certification to those interested in database deployment, performance, and management. Oracle is the largest provider of databases, and those certified through its program can expect increased competence, greater opportunities for advancement, more rewarding projects, and better pay. Candidates can obtain certification in various levels of database management, including associate, certified professional, and master.

Microsoft Certified Solutions Associate (MCSA) provides SQL Server accreditation. Students learn about the various certifications online and take courses at Microsoft training locations, high schools or colleges, or online through the company website.

Internships

In 2017, IT consultant TEKsystems surveyed 250 hiring managers across the United States. Eighty-six percent of these people said that internships were the most important thing they look for on the résumé of recent college graduates. Those who wish to work as database administrators should have no problem fulfilling this requirement. There is high demand for workers with DBA training, and numerous companies, large and small, offer internships to those who wish to pursue careers in database management. Internships provide prospective DBAs with hands-on experience and help a job candidate assemble a list of references. Job websites like LinkedIn and Glassdoor list hundreds of DBA intern opportunities for undergrads and recent college graduates.

Skills and Personality

Database administrators need good analytical skills to monitor database functions, fix problems, and prevent future failures. They need to be detail oriented to evaluate complex information and find minor glitches that can cause major problems. DBAs often work closely with development teams to assist in database design. Interacting with other tech professionals requires teamwork and communication skills. Good communication is also important when DBAs work with managers and other workers with fewer tech skills. And database management requires administrators to be self-motivated and ready to tackle new challenges. As Hawkins states: "If you're not self-motivated, guess what? You're going to find yourself in Section B where your office is somewhere in the basement."

Employers

Database administrators usually work for computer systems design companies. These enterprises design, implement, and manage database and other technology for businesses that do not have the internal resources to perform these duties themselves. Database administrators are also employed by education organizations, insurance carriers, and data processing companies. Some database administrators work for retail companies to keep track of customer credit card and shipping information. Those employed in the health care industry manage patient medical records. Almost every industry requires database administrators.

Working Conditions

Database administrators are committed to their jobs; they are often on call twenty-four hours a day and are sometimes required to perform updates and maintenance late at night when a database has fewer users or is off-line. In addition to mastering their technical duties, DBAs are expected to understand what businesses do with the data they collect, which can create a lot of pressure. Blogger Wendy Neu explains this factor on the Amazon Web Services website:

> Database administrators are under tremendous pressure every day to deliver value to the business across a variety of fronts. In general, a business's goals for using the data it gathers are to better understand the business, reduce costs, increase revenue, and deliver improvement and results. . . . The more time you spend in moving the business forward, the more likely that you will become a recognizable force for progress.

Earnings

According to the Bureau of Labor Statistics (BLS), the median annual wage for database administrators in 2016 was $84,950. The median wage is the wage at which half the workers in an occupation earned more than that amount and half earned less. The lowest 10 percent of database administrators earned less than $47,300, and the highest 10 percent earned more than $129,930.

Opportunities for Advancement

There are several types of database management systems (DBMS), including SQL, Oracle, and UNIX. Most employers use only one type and hire DBAs who are experienced and certified in their particular system. However, some companies use more than one database management system, and this provides advancement opportunities for those called "switchers": DBAs who can move between Oracle and SQL, for example. Those who understand several types of database management systems can expect better pay and more interesting assignments. On the Database Trends and Applications website, a database administrator named Craig S. offers advice for those who wish to become switchers:

> Find a company that uses both the [database management systems] you know and the DBMS you want to know. Apply for a position as a DBA for the DBMS you know and use the job . . . to get experience on the other DBMS. Once you have established yourself as a knowledgeable and effective DBA in the new shop, work your way over to help out [when] . . . the primary DBA goes on vacation. This way, you gain experience over time and do not have to abandon your current area of expertise.

Database administrators can also advance to become computer and information systems managers. These professionals, who plan, coordinate, and direct computer-related activities in an organization, earn an annual salary nearly twice as much as that of a DBA.

What Is the Future Outlook for Database Administrators?

As the amount of data continues to grow, companies in almost every economic sector are hiring database administrators to organize and manage data for analysts, customers, and other stakeholders. This is why the BLS predicts employment of database administrators will grow by 11 percent through 2026, faster than the average for all occupations. Growth will be even faster for DBAs who work for cloud computing firms that manage databases over the Internet. As more companies move their databases into the cloud, employment of DBAs in this sector is expected to grow by 17 percent through 2026.

Find Out More

Data Management Association International (DAMA)
364 E. Main St.
Middletown, DE 19709
website: https://dama.org

DAMA is a nonprofit international organization that provides an environment where data professionals can collaborate and communicate. The DAMA website section called "The Learning Channel" features webinars, certification programs, and other educational material for those interested in a career as a DBA.

EDM Council
website: www.edmcouncil.org

The Enterprise Data Management (EDM) Council is a trade association founded by the financial industry to make data management a business priority. The council hosts networking events and partners with eLearningCurve to deliver a number of e-learning, training, and certification programs.

IBM Professional Certification Program
1 New Orchard Rd.
Armonk, NY 10504
website: www-03.ibm.com/certify/index.shtml

This website offers several levels of official IBM database administrator certification to students and those employed as DBAs. Site visitors can find prep materials and take the exams necessary for certification as database administrators.

Oracle University
website: http://education.oracle.com

The Oracle Corporation, which specializes in database management software and technology, offers training and certification through its Oracle University website. Students can learn about database warehousing, application development, and MySQL.

Computer Systems Analyst

Computer Systems Analyst

Minimum Educational Requirements
Bachelor's degree

Personal Qualities
Analytical; creative; critical thinker; good communication, reading, and writing skills; problem solver

Certification and Licensing
Microsoft, Oracle, and other manufacturers offer certification in their systems

Working Conditions
Full-time, indoors, in constant collaboration with others

Salary
$87,220 median annual pay in 2016

Number of Jobs
600,500 in 2016

Future Job Outlook
9 percent growth through 2026

What Does a Computer Systems Analyst Do?

Most businesses depend on computer systems for e-mail, data processing, design, research, sales, bookkeeping, and numerous other tasks. Centralized computer systems are often connected to multiple employee workstations, mobile networks, printers, scanners, and additional equipment. As any computer user knows, software, hardware, and other parts of the system do not always function properly. Additionally, software needs to be updated regularly while hardware is upgraded as technology changes.

As the job title implies, computer systems analysts are in charge of analyzing computer systems. Their thorough understanding of computer software and hardware allows them to enhance system performance. Computer systems analysts simplify methods workers can use to share information, fix glitches and crashes, and perform regular maintenance and upgrades. They conduct detailed tests and analyze trends in data flow to plan for memory and speed updates.

While technical knowledge is an important aspect of the job, computer systems analysts are required to merge their IT talents with business skills. Successful computer systems analysts possess a comprehensive understanding of their employer's business whether it be a financial firm or an engineering company. As blogger Jess Mansour Scherman writes on the Rasmussen College website: "Computer systems analysts . . . must maintain perfect harmony between an organization's personnel, [business practices,] and computer systems. In order to sustain this balance, they must retain a holistic understanding of the organization and how each component works together."

Computer systems analysts use their business acumen to research, evaluate, and recommend new technologies for their employers. They prepare cost-benefit analysis so management can decide whether IT systems and computing infrastructure upgrades are worthwhile financially. When equipment purchases are made, computer systems analysts work to get the best deals from vendors and to ensure their employers receive the most efficient and cost-effective technology.

Computer systems analysts are often specialists who focus on specific aspects of the job. Those individuals who supervise every aspect of computer system installation and upgrades are called IT project managers. These professionals monitor a project at every step to ensure budgets, deadlines, and company standards are met. IT project managers might also oversee a company's entire information technology department where they supervise employees and take an active role in the recruitment process.

Some computer systems analysts are known as software quality assurance (QA) analysts. These specialists are testers and problem solvers who perform in-depth analysis of websites and software. They search for glitches, document issues, and correct errors. After problems are fixed, software QA analysts return to the program and test it again, searching for vulnerabilities that users might encounter.

Programmer analysts spend their days writing computer code to create custom business applications for their employer. They code more than other analysts, debugging apps and addressing specific business problems with their applications.

How Do You Become a Computer Systems Analyst?

Education

In 2016 labor market analyst Burning Glass Technologies examined nearly 119,000 job postings for "computer systems analyst." The study found that 84 percent of employers that hire computer systems analysts require job candidates to hold a bachelor's degree or higher in a computer-related field. The most common degrees are a bachelor of science in computer science or IT management. Because of the business aspect of the job, prospective computer systems analysts will find it helpful to take business courses.

Some employers prefer computer systems analysts to hold a master's degree in business administration (MBA) with a concentration in IT systems. Those with the most complex computer systems require job candidates to have a master's degree in computer science.

The learning process continues for computer systems analysts as long as they are working in the field. Technology changes rapidly, and as IT professor P.K. Agarwal writes on the TechSpective website: "Anyone who stops advancing [his or her] career education will quickly become sidelined in such a fast-paced market. To stay relevant, [computer systems analysts] should continually seek to reskill and upskill themselves through the ongoing development of new technical proficiencies, and by expanding their professional networks."

Certification and Licensing

Computer systems analysts who attain certification can expect higher wages, better job opportunities, and greater chances for advancement. Most certification programs are run by vendors like Microsoft, Oracle, and others that manufacture computer systems software and hardware. Computer systems analysts can visit those company websites to find certification programs that are right for them. The Institute for Certification of Computing Professionals (ICCP) offers Information Systems Analyst (ISA) Certification to aspiring computer systems analysts who have graduated from four-year degree programs. Those who score 70 percent or higher across each of the three ICCP exams receive the ISA-Masters title. These experts can enroll in the Trainer certification program and, after passing the exam, obtain the ISA-Principal certification.

Internships

Employers generally prefer to hire computer systems analysts with two or more years of experience. But many accept those analysts who have completed internships that provided them with hands-on development experience and knowledge of hardware and software systems. Internships provide excellent networking opportunities, and interns often find mentors who are willing to help them learn. On the business magazine *Fast Company*'s website, Michael Grothaus, who attended Stanford University, describes the benefits of his internship at Google:

> My manager was fantastic at both mentoring me during my projects and allowing me the freedom to learn independently. . . . Academically, working for a technology company motivated me to pursue a master's degree in computer science. . . . My interactions with the engineering team, and the business team within a technology company, helped me recognize the importance of a degree.

Skills and Personality

In addition to their tech skills, computer systems analysts must possess what are called soft skills, or personal qualities that will help them find success in the workplace. As one might expect from the job title, computer systems analysts need to be very analytical. They must absorb large amounts of data and mentally process complex information to perform their job.

Problem-solving and critical-thinking skills work together to help a computer systems analyst to identify a problem and evaluate solutions to find the proper remedy. Multitasking skills are important for computer systems analysts who need to remain organized and focused while dealing with numerous problems.

Good communication skills are a must as computer systems analysts work with engineers, programmers, management teams, and others. Good communication means expressing complex ideas clearly in plain English and listening closely to the comments, suggestions, and questions posed by others. Communication extends to writing since computer systems analysts are required to publish weekly progress reports and other documents.

Computer systems analysts also need to be good readers who can learn from manuals, technical journals, and periodicals. Reading helps analysts identify new design tools, implement technology, and keep up with changes in the industry.

Another important skill might surprise those who envision a stereotypical nerd as the perfect computer systems analyst. According to an unnamed source on the Princeton Review website:

> One of the biggest surprises in my 25 years of technology work is that people who have a creative background as opposed to a degree in computer science tend to make better systems analysts. The best analysts I've come across came from backgrounds in theater, art, and filmmaking. But they were all able to see and grasp big-picture concepts very quickly, and break them down into subcomponents. People who have a computer science or math background tend to be very technical, and sometimes that can be a hindrance.

Employers

Computer systems analysts can be found at nearly every major corporation from Silicon Valley on the West Coast to Wall Street on the East Coast. Computer systems analysts work for computer systems design firms, science companies, health care providers, and banking, finance, and insurance corporations. Around 6 percent of the 600,500 computer analysts working in the field in 2016 were employed by local, state, and federal government agencies.

Working Conditions

In 2018 *U.S. News & World Report* announced the best jobs for the year, and computer systems analyst was rated as number four in the Best Technology jobs category. But those who work in analyzing computer systems can expect challenges. Around 20 percent of those in the profession work more than forty hours per week.

Computer systems analysts need to remain focused on minute details for long periods of time. They must also be prepared to quickly shift from one task to the next. On a typical workday a computer systems analyst will test, maintain, and monitor computer programs and systems, review and scrutinize computer printouts to locate code problems, and develop new programs for clients. Computer systems analysts solve problems for less experienced staff, attend management meetings, and work with engineers and programmers to expand or modify systems. As *U.S. News* notes about the ranking: "You'll find far more extroverts in this field than in other IT jobs, since the job duties include near-constant collaboration with others."

Earnings

The main reason computer systems analyst ranked so high with *U.S. News & World Report* is the salary. According to the Bureau of Labor Statistics (BLS), the median annual wage for computer systems analysts was $87,220 in 2016; those in the highest 10 percent earned more than $137,690. Further, a computer systems analyst can earn a great living with little experience. According to one employer quoted on the Princeton Review website in 2018: "I have a position available for someone with two years' experience. I can't get anyone for less than $80,000 and the position is still open."

Opportunities for Advancement

Computer systems analysts just starting out in the field will work on details contained within small sections of large systems. After about five years of experience, they can expect to manage entire projects that involve applications, machinery, networks, and user communities. After ten years in the field, a computer systems analyst might be placed in charge of an entire technology department or be promoted to chief technology officer. These professionals earn salaries well into six figures. Computer systems analysts can also earn $125 per hour or more working as consultants.

> ### What Is the Future Outlook for Computer Systems Analysts?

The BLS predicts employment of computer systems analysts will grow by 9 percent through 2026 as companies throughout the economy increase their reliance on information technology. Computer systems analysts will be hired by contractors who provide cloud services to smaller firms that do not have their own IT departments. Additional job growth is expected in the health care sector as providers hire computer systems analysts to help with electronic health records, online diagnoses systems, and other health care–related IT.

Find Out More

Association of Information Technology Professionals (AITP)
3500 Lacey Rd.
Downers Grove, IL 60515
website: www.aitp.org

The AITP, also known as CompTIA, is a professional organization with 62 local chapters and 286 student chapters at colleges and universities. The association offers webinars, conferences, and job listings to members; and its student program connects students to mentors and provides résumé support and career strategies.

The Institute for Certification of Computer Professionals (ICCP)
2400 E. Devon Ave.
Des Plaines, IL 60018
website: www.iccp.org

The ICCP provides computer and data analysts with certification, education, and a professional code of ethics. The institute accredits universities, provides curriculum, and offers numerous courses of value to computer systems analysts.

Software Engineering Institute (SEI)
4500 Fifth Ave.
Pittsburgh, PA 15213
website: www.sei.cmu.edu

SEI works to help government and industry acquire, develop, operate, and sustain software systems that are innovative, affordable, and secure. The SEI website offers training and career advice and features an online library and certification programs.

Tech Dev Guide
website: https://techdevguide.withgoogle.com

This website hosted by Google is intended to provide tips and resources to university-level computer science students seeking internships. The site features "Google's Guide to Technical Development" with tools aimed at experienced programmers and advanced students.

Information Security Analyst

Information Security Analyst

Minimum Educational Requirements
Bachelor's degree

Personal Qualities
Eye for detail, analytical, problem-solving skills, hard worker, comprehensive IT knowledge

Certification and Licensing
Certified Information Systems Security Professional (CISSP)

Working Conditions
Full-time employment with occasional long hours and high-stress situations

Salary
$92,600 median annual wage in 2016

Number of Jobs
100,000 in 2016

Future Job Outlook
28 percent growth through 2026

What Does an Information Security Analyst Do?

A typical business organization has a computer network with a website on the Internet that is open to the public. The website allows customers to pick a username and password, which allows them to access parts of the company's computer network. Customers can purchase goods, check on orders, contact sales personnel, and perform other tasks.

Digital firewalls prevent customers from accessing other parts of a company's internal network that contain secure information only available to employees. This is the area in which a company runs into cybersecurity problems. Hackers use various means to breach firewalls to illegally access a company's internal databases, which often contain names, addresses, passwords, credit card

41

numbers, and other critical data. Sometimes hacks make headlines like in 2017 when hackers stole personal and financial data on 145 million people from the databases of the consumer credit rating company Equifax.

While big hacks make headlines, a new type of threat, called a ransomware attack, is rarely noted in the press. When a ransomware attack occurs, a hacker locks up a company's data with encryption software so that it cannot be accessed by employees. To free the network, hackers demand a ransom that might range from a few hundred to a few million dollars. According to the FBI, over four thousand ransomware attacks occurred in 2016—more than ten a day.

The professionals who act as the digital police force on the Internet are known as information security analysts. These people, often referred to as infosec analysts, constantly monitor networks for security breaches. They also run simulated attacks to search for network vulnerabilities. Information security analysts install software such as firewalls and data encryption programs to protect networks and develop security standards to protect their clients. Information security analyst Gaurav S. explains his role on the information-sharing website Quora: "Information Security Analysts are frontline warriors . . . who observe and report any security breach incidents happening or [that have] happened at their respective organization."

Information security analysts must remain up-to-date on the latest IT security trends and inform their clients about important security procedures. As information technology professor Kevin Hawkins puts it on the Cyber Security website: "You have to be on top of the latest and greatest technology or you're not going to survive."

While information security analysts work to protect networks, they are also in charge of ensuring that data is regularly backed up to an off-site location. They create disaster recovery plans to be implemented in case of an emergency, including procedures employees must follow to allow their organization to continue operations. Information security analysts create plans to restore proper IT functions after a hack and test the plans regularly.

Information security analysts must understand highly complex information to perform their jobs. They need to understand firewalls, network security, system and network configuration, and TCP (Transmission Control Protocol). Knowledge of operating systems such as UNIX, Linux, and Windows is important. Information security analysts are experts in encryption techniques that prevent third parties from reading private messages. And they have to be familiar with a law called the Cybersecurity Information Sharing Act (CISA) that requires companies to share information about cyberattacks with the federal government.

How Do You Become an Information Security Analyst?

Education

Infosec analysts perform complex, highly technical tasks. According to an employment study by Burning Glass Technologies, nearly 90 percent of those who work as infosec specialists hold at least a bachelor's degree. Prospective information security analysts major in computer science, information technology, or computer systems security/information assurance. Some employers require their information security analysts to have a master of science degree in cybersecurity or digital forensic science.

Those who major in computer science study computer theory, computing problems and solutions, and the design of computer systems and user interfaces. Information technology majors focus on IT system design, business and research data programs, and communications support. Programs that teach computer systems security/information assurance include a wide range of subjects related to computer and network security systems, including computer architecture, cryptography, contingency planning, investigation techniques, networking laws and regulations, risk assessment, systems analysis, and security system design.

As the demand for information security analysts continues to grow, many more schools are working to meet the challenge of providing these specialized courses. As cybersecurity specialist Mari Galloway writes on the Infosecurity website: "Colleges and universities are . . . stepping up their game to ensure they provide adequate training and knowledge to those wanting to enter the field. These institutions are using skilled professionals to help build out these programs to include hands-on activities, labs, and interpersonal skills necessary to be successful."

Certification

Certification as a cybersecurity professional serves as a badge of approval in the world of information technology. And those who hold certifications can expect higher wages. According to the *2017 Global Information Security Workforce Study*, information security employees with certification report earning salaries that are 35 percent higher than noncertified workers.

There are several popular certifications for information security analysts that raise the holder's credibility, improve job security, and create new opportunities. The Certified Information Systems Security Professional (CISSP) is the most widely recognized accreditation in the cybersecurity industry. The Center for Cyber Safety and Education is a leading provider of CISSP certification. CISSP certification covers eight domains: security and risk management, asset security, security engineering, communications and network security, identity and access management, security assessment and training, security operations, and software development security.

Internships and Hackathons

The path to becoming an information security analyst can be a long one, and most companies do not hire those individuals who have not acquired experience as interns. The FBI Cyber Internship program is recognized as one of the most prestigious for hopeful information security students. The program is open to undergraduate, graduate, or postdoctoral students throughout the nation. Interns can work at FBI field offices or the agency's headquarters in Washington, DC. The ten-week summer program places interns in various FBI departments, including the Cyber Division, Operational Technology Division, and Informational Technology Branch, as well as the divisions of Counterintelligence, Counterterrorism, and Criminal Intrusion.

Another way prospective information security analysts can gain experience is through conferences sometimes referred to as hackathons. These hackathons often last up to twenty-four hours. Participants compete to attack or defend computers and networks from cybersecurity threats. These events are fun, educational, and provide experience that looks good on a résumé. As contributing editor to *Infosecurity Magazine* Dan Raywood explains: "I highly recommend anyone to attend a hackathon and work on a project of their choice, something they are really passionate about. [Hackathons] are great to just force you and some pals to sit down for 24 hours and just work on something. It is all self-taught."

Skills and Personality

It takes a lot of hard work, passion, and determination to become an information security analyst, as security consultant Ryan Hausknecht explains on the *Infosecurity Magazine* website: "Breaking into infosec is not something easy; it's one of the hottest fields out there and has a very high learning curve, with the addition of a need to know how everything in IT works. . . . You need to know how everything comes together, both on the networking side and system administrative side."

In order to "know how everything in IT works," information security analysts require strong problem-solving and analytical skills. They need to closely study the strengths and weaknesses found in their employer's computer systems and networks. Paying close attention to details is necessary since cyberattacks can be extremely difficult to detect; even minor changes in network performance can signal that an attack is under way. Creative thinking helps information security analysts stay one step ahead of hackers and allows the analysts to understand hackers' motives and methods.

On the Job

Employers

The demand for infosec warriors is exploding at a rapid rate due to the unprecedented frequency of cyberattacks. This means information security analysts are in demand from coast to coast in nearly all economic sectors. As Julie Peeler, director of the Center for Cyber Safety and Education, notes: "Having qualified cybersecurity professionals is critical in all industries. Employers must act quickly to close workforce gaps and mitigate the risks that threaten enterprises."

Working Conditions

Information security analysts are the first line of defense against cyberattacks, and they need to be alert and vigilant at all times. The job involves monitoring a security dashboard that provides information about the online activities of key individuals and websites within an organization. The stakes are high, and the work can be very stressful. As Larry Shoup, founder of the cybersecurity firm ClearArmor Corporation, told *Forbes* in 2017: "[Hackers] are talented, they are organized, they are tenacious, they are very good at figuring out how to attack you and monetize your misfortune. People used to think of hackers as kids in their garages with something to prove, but these are organized businesses now."

Meetings are also a constant fact of infosec life. Security personnel meet with audit teams that perform security reviews for a company's clients. Implementation teams meet to discuss security problems and fixes for various projects. Emergency meetings are held when security breaches are found. Information security professionals also meet with corporate executives to explain—in plain English—the benefits of security programs. As infosec professor Kevin Jones explains in an article for *Infosecurity Magazine*: "The [security analyst's] real job is to interface between those at the business end of the organization, and those at the technical end. It has been hard to find people who could go in front of the board and explain why they need to spend a boatload of money on making the company more secure."

Earnings

According to the Bureau of Labor Statistics (BLS), the median annual wage for information security analysts was $92,600 in 2016. This wage is the wage at which half the workers in an occupation earned more than that amount and half earned less. The lowest 10 percent of information security analysts earned less than $53,760, and the highest 10 percent earned more than $147,290.

Opportunities for Advancement

Most people do not become information security analysts straight out of college. The work is so critical that most employers require job candidates to have at least two years of experience. Likewise, it can take a long time to advance to more senior security roles. Hausknecht describes his career arc: "I started as an intern . . . and dealt with managing servers that ran the security systems on hydro plants, coal plants, power plants, etc. From there I was promoted to system administrator where I got a lot of networking and system administrative experience. From there I moved to a security engineer role for a short while until I moved into a security analyst role."

What Is the Future Outlook for Information Security Analysts?

According to the BLS, employment of information security analysts is projected to grow by 28 percent through 2026. That's four times the average growth rate for all occupations. Banks and financial institutions will be among the leading employers of information security analysts, followed by health care providers and tech corporations. The BLS predicts that employment of information security analysts will grow at an astounding 56 percent through 2026 at companies that provide cloud services for small- and medium-sized businesses.

Find Out More

Center for Cyber Safety and Education
311 Park Place Blvd.
Clearwater, FL 33759
website: https://iamcybersafe.org

This nonprofit charitable trust specializes in vendor-neutral training and certification for cybersecurity professionals. The center provides educational materials for parents, children, and teachers, as well as scholarships aimed at women, undergrads, and graduate students.

Infosecurity Magazine
website: www.infosecurity-magazine.com

This e-publication contains hundreds of articles about the information security industry, including current events and topics ranging from application security to encryption and malware. The magazine's Next-Gen section allows prospective information security analysts to publish research, work, and blog posts.

SANS Institute
8120 Woodmont Ave.
Bethesda, MD 20814
website: www.sans.org

The SANS Institute is a research and educational organization focused on immersive computer security training and certification. The institute offers training in classroom settings throughout the world and also offers on-demand, live, and simulcast programs over the Internet.

Women's Society of Cyberjutsu (WSC)
1405 S. Fern St.
Arlington, VA 22202
website: https://womenscyberjutsu.org

The Women's Society of Cyberjutsu works to empower women in the cybersecurity field. The organization provides hands-on technical training and workshops. The Cyberjutsu Girls Academy sponsors a once-a-month STEM- and security-related program for girls aged twelve through fifteen.

Software Developer

What Does a Software Developer Do?

Whether you are listening to music on your laptop, playing a computer game on your smartphone, posting pictures on social media, or streaming a movie on your TV, you are using applications created by software developers. These creative geniuses develop apps that allow people to perform numerous tasks on computers and other digital devices, from balancing a checkbook to booking a flight around the world. Beyond specific apps, software developers write software that runs almost all the machinery used in daily life, including dishwashers, televisions, cars, and even rockets and spacecraft.

Software developers invent new ways to perform a digital task or analyze user needs and design, test, and develop software programs to meet those needs. After software developers create an application or new piece of software, they analyze and test it to ensure it is working perfectly. Performance and security functions are added depending on the needs of the client. Software developers then create models, instructions, and diagrams called

At a Glance

Software Developer

Minimum Educational Requirements
Bachelor's degree

Personal Qualities
Problem solver, analytical thinker, team player, good communication and reading skills

Certification and Licensing
Certified Secure Software Lifecycle Professional (CSSLP)

Working Conditions
Full-time employment with long hours at complex tasks and a high level of social interaction

Salary
$102,280 annual median wage in 2016

Number of Jobs
1,256,200 in 2016

Future Job Outlook
24 percent growth through 2026

flowcharts for programmers to write code and further test the software. And software developers document every aspect of the software as a reference for future upgrades.

Newly created software can have bugs or be difficult to use. Failure is part of the job, and software developers need to deal with disappointment. As software developer Amanda Smith notes in an interview on the Pearson Education website: "I distinctly remember the day I released my first bug to our production environment. I felt like such a failure and I was so embarrassed! . . . I shed a few tears at my desk and debated throwing away my entire development career that day. It took me awhile to realize that the small mistakes are what I could learn the most from. Mistakes are just a part of the job." When mistakes are discovered, software developers go back through the design process to fix problems and improve software functions. Once the software is released to the public, the developer needs to follow up on reviews, comments, and complaints to further refine it.

Some software developers are specialists who focus on specific aspects of the job. Application software developers, as the name implies, focus on computer applications designed for individual users. These developers create games, word processors, photography apps, financial software, databases, and countless other applications. The products may be sold to the public or developed for individual businesses, organizations, and other entities according to their needs.

Systems software developers create computer operating systems. They create software programs that perform basic functions for computers, cell phones, tablets, video game systems, e-readers, and other consumer electronics. These programs run in the background but are not developed for individual users.

Developers who oversee the complete creation of an app or systems software from planning stages through distribution are called IT project managers. In addition to developing the software, they are responsible for meeting budgets, deadlines, and quality standards.

How Do You Become a Software Developer?

Education

Most software developers have a bachelor's degree in computer science, software engineering, or a related field. Computer science degree programs are considered the most helpful because the courses cover topics such as software design, information and database systems, operating systems, and data structures and algorithms.

Prospective software developers can make high school count by taking as many math courses as possible, including calculus, trigonometry, and algebra. Computer science courses that emphasize programming languages are helpful, as are classes in physics and communications.

Some students who master coding in high school can find work without attending college. As Stephen Sinco of the *Coding Dojo Blog* explains:

> Believe it or not, but there's a significant population of software developers in the tech-industry who are self-taught and . . . don't have formal degrees. This is because computer programming is a trade, and it can be taught in the same manner that someone can learn how to use Adobe Photoshop or Illustrator. . . . Additionally, many programming technologies such as PHP are extensively documented online and are enthusiastically supported by the online community, which further promotes opportunities for self-taught coding.

Another way for students interested in software development to learn and acquire coding skills is by participating in programming puzzle websites like CodeKata and TopCoder. These websites attract highly skilled coders who compete to solve problems while sharing notes and methods after problems are solved. The nearly one million members of the TopCoder community provide different areas of expertise, according to website founder Jack Hughes:

Some folks are really good at finding bugs and they'll come in and they'll just do that. Some folks are really good at fixing bugs; they'll come in and just do that. [Some] might have been fixing bugs yesterday and today they want to learn software design, so they'll come in and start competing in that. . . . They don't think they can win at first—but what they're going to get is [a] tremendous amount of feedback about how well they do it.

Certification

Cybersecurity threats are increasing at a rapid rate, and hackers often take advantage of security loopholes that software developers accidently leave in their source code. Software developers who earn the Certified Secure Software Lifecycle Professional (CSSLP) certification assure their employers that they possess the latest information about keeping software safe. The CSSLP is a vendor-neutral credential awarded by the International Information System Security Certification Consortium, or (ISC)^2. Those who earn the certificate learn the most up-to-date security practices used in software design, implementation, testing, and deployment.

Internships

Whether a software developer is self-taught, went to code camp, or is a graduate of a major university, an internship will provide some of the vital experience that hiring managers look for on a résumé. Software developer interns learn how to work on projects from start to finish and develop the analytical thinking skills necessary for a successful career. Interns work with mentors who share knowledge and experience. Software developer Hesham, who interned for EventMobi, an events management platform company, describes the insights he gained: "EventMobi holds monthly engineering lightning talks where members of the engineering team give 5–10 minute presentations on particular areas of expertise. Their talks serve as primers to a variety of topics and have been extremely beneficial to me as an intern."

Skills and Personality

Software developers are problem solvers who enjoy analyzing a program and figuring out new ways to make life easier for computer users. Those who work in the field tend to be strategic thinkers, as blogger Lauren Elrick explains on the Rasmussen College website: "If you're someone who likes solving a mystery by looking at the big picture as well as the smaller steps along the way, you'll be right at home developing software. There's a lot of planning that goes into these types of programs, and if you can figure out the fastest path from point A to point B, the world of software development will welcome you with open arms."

Software developers need to stay informed about changes in technology. Many start their day catching up on software tools, languages, and techniques, which are constantly evolving. Some companies pay for their developers to have access to an online developer training library that features courses on new technology.

While software developers need great tech skills, they need people skills as well. Software developers work with programmers, computer engineers, business and marketing executives, and other nontechnical personnel. Good communication and listening skills are important. Communication skills are also important for reaching out to others when problems arise, as Smith explains: "Talk to other developers in the field. . . . The most effective way for me to learn something new has always been to talk to someone in the industry."

On the Job

Employers

Approximately 1.2 million software developers were employed in 2016. And with the constant demand for new applications, software developers are finding work across a broad range of industries. Application software developers work for software publishing companies along with those that manufacture smartphones and computer hardware. They also find employment in heavily tech-reliant industries such as banking, insurance, health care, and manufacturing.

Systems software developers are seeing new opportunities as more manufacturers incorporate computers into everything from self-driving cars to voice-command trash cans. The growing threat posed by hackers is also providing work for systems software developers who are creating software to protect computer systems, networks, and digital infrastructure.

Working Conditions

Software developers generally work forty-hour weeks but can expect to work overtime when deadlines loom. Most begin their days going through e-mails from clients and users who need guidance or have discovered problems with an application or software system. Meetings are another major part of the workday, as software developers often work in teams that follow a task list that might include conducting research into a problem and meeting with business teams to discuss the financial parameters of a project as well as writing code.

Software developer Christi Ward-Waller, who works in the benefits department of American Fidelity Insurance, defines an important aspect of her job on the Chegg Internships website:

> I truly believe that even as a software developer my job is to make someone else's life happy. If I can find a new way for them to do their processes that will improve their lives, make their documents go faster, make their day go faster and easier, find something that they don't have to do manually anymore and I can automate that for them, I love that. . . . I wake up in the morning and can't wait to get to work because I am problem-solving, I am learning constantly, it's a very creative job.

Earnings

According to the Bureau of Labor Statistics (BLS), the median annual wage for software developers in 2016 was $102,280.

The highest 10 percent of software developers earned more than $157,590 while the lowest 10 percent earned less than $58,300. Software publishers paid application software developers the highest median wage, around $111,000, while computer systems designers paid around $98,000. Manufacturers paid $117,360, the best median wage for systems software developers.

Opportunities for Advancement

Software developers with five to ten years of experience can advance to the role of information technology project manager or information systems manager. In this position they oversee the complete software development process. Some software developers start their own companies as the need for new applications and other software grows exponentially. A few of these entrepreneurs have gone on to great wealth and fame as the most influential software developers of all time. Facebook founder Mark Zuckerberg began developing software while still in high school. Bill Gates established his reputation as a software developer in high school and went on to found Microsoft, one of the world's most successful software companies.

What Is the Future Outlook for Software Developers?

The exploding demand in nearly every economic sector for new computer software is responsible for the bright job outlook for software developers. The BLS predicts that demand for software developers will grow by 24 percent through 2026, more than four times the rate for all jobs. Those who specialize as applications developers will see even more opportunities; employment is projected to grow by 30 percent by 2026. Demand for systems developers will be slower, with such employment expected to grow by 11 percent.

Find Out More

Association of Software Professionals (ASP)
PO Box 1522
Martinsville, IN 46151
website: http://asp-software.org

This organization is made up of independent software developers who have created freeware and shareware. Students can access the ASP to learn from successful developers of desktop and laptop programs and cloud computing and mobile apps.

Institute of Electrical and Electronics Engineers (IEEE)
website: www.ieee.org

The IEEE offers students a wide range of learning, career, and employment opportunities. The organization's Standards University offers courses, games, videos, an e-magazine, and an e-learning library. In addition, the IEEE provides certifications for computer professionals.

Software Development Forum
111 W. Saint John St.
San Jose, CA 95113
website: www.sdforum.org

The Software Development Forum is based in Silicon Valley and holds around twenty-five events monthly that are attended by engineers, developers, entrepreneurs, and tech experts. The forum provides information, education, and connections for those seeking to build a career in Silicon Valley.

TopCoder
website: www.topcoder.com

This website with nearly one million highly skilled members hosts bimonthly computer programming contests in which software developers, designers, and student programmers compete for cash prizes while solving real computing problems.

Computer Network Architect

At a Glance

At a Glance

Computer Network Architect

Minimum Educational Requirements
Bachelor's degree

Personal Qualities
Analytical, detail oriented, good interpersonal skills, business acumen

Certification
Cisco Certified Design Expert (CCDE) and Cisco Certified Architect (CCAr)

Working Conditions
Full-time work with some overtime required

Salary
$101,210 median annual wage in 2016

Number of Jobs
162,700 in 2016

Future Job Outlook
6 percent growth through 2026

What Does a Computer Network Architect Do?

The word *architect* is traditionally associated with people who plan and design buildings. Architects are familiar with construction materials like concrete, wood, and glass, and they understand how these materials fit together to form a sound structure. In the tech world the term *architect* refers to builders of computer networks. These professionals plan, design, and construct data communication networks that range from small intranets used in private organizations to extensive cloud systems. Computer network architects build with materials such as computers, servers, routers, network drivers, cables, and software programs. They draw on their expertise in telecommunications to create local area networks (LANs), wide area networks (WANs), Internet portals, and e-mail networks.

The job of a traditional architect is finished when a building is completed, but the work of computer network architects is ongoing. These technical experts spend their days overseeing firmware updates, analyzing data traffic on the networks, monitoring for security breaches, and planning for future network growth. When expansions or changes are required, computer network architects use network modeling software to build test networks, which are analyzed, tested, and perfected.

Computer network architects rarely work alone. They share their research with managers and work with company executives to plan upgrades and install new equipment. Computer network architects interact with consultants, outside vendors, and financial, marketing, and technical personnel.

David Lef, the principal computer network architect for Microsoft IT, oversees one of the most complex and extensive networks ever created. The Microsoft IT network features networking components that connect 220,000 employees and vendors to nine hundred locations around the world. Lef describes his job on the Microsoft Azure website:

> Our network supports over 2,500 individual applications and business processes. We are responsible for providing wired, wireless, and remote network access for the organization, implementing network security across our network, and [ensuring] that the nuts and bolts of network functionality work as they should: IP addressing, name resolution, traffic management, switching, routing, and so on.

How Do You Become a Computer Network Architect?

Education

Computer network architects need at least a bachelor's degree in computer science, information systems, mathematics, physics, or engineering. High school students considering a career as a computer network architect should take math courses, including calculus, trigonometry, and algebra. Computer science courses that emphasize coding, physics, and communications are also helpful. And, according to network architect Bryian Winner, industrial arts courses can be extremely useful. Students in industrial arts classes use a variety of hand, power, and machine tools to fabricate objects from wood and metal. As Winner states in an interview on the Chegg Internships website: "You have to be able to understand how things are built to be able to work with them."

Employers of computer network architects sometimes require applicants to have a master of business administration (MBA) in information systems. Obtaining an MBA requires an additional two years of study in business and computer-related courses.

While education is important for becoming a computer network architect, most graduates will not begin working in this role right out of school. Employers typically require five to ten years of experience in related fields such as database administration, computer systems analysis, or network administration. As Winner explains, the majority of computer network architects "have some formalized education but much of it is learned in the field and it almost works like an apprenticeship. You'll work with other IT people and see how they develop the networks."

Computer network architects, like other IT professionals, constantly update their knowledge. They read the latest tech articles, attend conferences, and take classes to stay informed about the latest changes in technology. As professor of computer science Peter Steenkiste tells *U.S. News & World Report*: "You will have to constantly learn. You need to be very much aware of not just the technologies available today but about the trends. A lot of the designing of networks is effectively upgrading and expanding the networks."

Certification

Computer network architects can expect higher salaries, better job assignments, and greater chances for promotions as they advance up the certification ladder. The process starts with basic certifications and moves up to more complex certifications.

Computer network architects design and build data communication networks, both small and large. They work with computers, servers, routers, network drivers, cables, and software programs during their design-and-build projects.

For example, the Cisco Certified Design Associate (CCDA) and Cisco Certified Design Professional (CCDP) certifications can lead to jobs in networking and cloud infrastructure. This type of employment provides experience to those hoping to advance to the position of computer network architect. Once this goal is achieved, computer network architects can continue up the certification ladder by obtaining the Cisco Certified Design Expert (CCDE) certification, which is a prerequisite for the Cisco Certified Architect (CCAr) certification. At this level, a computer network architect can also obtain certifications in Cisco Certified Internetwork Expert (CCIE), Routing and Switching, or Data Center. Other senior network architect certifications include Salesforce Certified Technical Architect (CTA) and Red Hat Certified Architect (RHCA).

Internships

Most high-paying jobs in the tech industry require more than a college degree. Job recruiters are looking for those individuals with previous experience as an intern or employee. This is particularly true for computer network architects who often work in related fields before landing their jobs. Anyone who wishes to become a computer network architect should seek an internship program that focuses on computer, network, or database administration. Professors often link students to internships, but positions can be obtained by e-mailing the numerous tech companies that offer internship programs.

Skills and Personality

For computer network architects, the ability to collaborate with others is as important as knowing the intricate technical aspects of a complex network. Miscommunication with team members and poor relations with vendors can cause critical networks to fail. As network systems consultant James Stanger points out on the Tech-Target website: "What you find is that there's a tremendous amount of work involved in keeping those systems updated and monitored, and then monitoring the service providers you've called in."

Computer network architects need to be analytical and detail oriented. They have to create comprehensive plans for networks and closely examine network functions. Organizational skills are necessary when creating precisely functioning networks from multiple parts. Computer network architects also need strong business acumen. The overriding job of a computer network architect is to match the most cost-effective and efficient hardware and software with a company's long-term business goals. This task requires a comprehensive understanding of an employer's business plans, budgets, and objectives.

While these skills are important, most employers are willing to train computer network architects on the most up-to-date procedures and equipment. And technical ability alone no longer ensures entry into a top job. Employers are less willing to hire someone who lacks soft skills that include tact, the ability to communicate clearly, and leadership skills. As network architect Lee

Badman tells TechTarget: "There's a lot of diplomacy. There are a lot of meetings with people who either know what they want and you have to help them translate that into a technical solution, or who think they know what they want and you can see that it's never going to work. You have to diplomatically and nicely help them find the solution and abandon their crazy idea."

Computer systems architects need to be self-educators who are willing to take advice and acquire knowledge from others. Winner explains, "If you don't know how [to do something], say you don't know and ask. Learn anything and everything you can get your hands on. . . . The more you know the more you can do. The more you can do the more valuable you become."

On the Job

Employers

In 2017 many companies were having difficulties filling computer network architect positions because of the considerable education and work experience requirements. IT recruiter Dan Scandalito tells TechTarget: "People at the architect level are sought after, and there's not much talent that's available." Employers seeking computer network architects include telecommunications carriers, insurance companies, computer systems design firms, educational institutions, and government agencies.

Working Conditions

Computer network architects work full-time, but the job can be demanding and require additional hours spent on the job. According to the Bureau of Labor Statistics (BLS), about one in four computer network architects worked more than forty hours per week in 2016. For those who love IT, the job provides a chance to consistently play around with shiny new tech tools (new systems can cost up to $600,000). But computer network architects also need to show restraint; the equipment they purchase has to address real business needs. As senior network architect Bill Dugger explains on the TechTarget website: "You have to architect for a purpose, whether it's to reduce a hardware footprint or to streamline an application flow. You have to look at how the company you're architecting for does its business."

Whatever the case the job is very fulfilling, as network architect Kyle Cooper tells TechTarget: "The biggest thing that's rewarding is you really do make a big impact on the systems and infrastructure of an organization. The other [rewarding] aspect is you're constantly researching and learning new technologies and systems. [The job is perfect] for people who are passionate about IT systems."

Earnings

According to the BLS, the median annual wage for computer network architects in 2016 was $101,210. Those in the lowest 10 percent earned around $55,610, while computer network architects receiving the highest pay earned more than $158,500. Computer network architects who worked for telecommunications companies like Verizon, AT&T, or Sprint earned above the median wage, around $107,000 annually in 2016. Those who were employed by state, local, and private educational institutions brought in a lower wage of $62,390.

Opportunities for Advancement

A computer network architect is already in an advanced position professionally. Some architects advance to the position of computer and information systems manager, a job commonly referred to as an IT manager. These highly paid professionals can earn more than $135,000 annually by planning, coordinating, and directing a company's digital activities. Computer network architects can also move up to executive positions like chief technology officer (CTO), a job that involves determining the overall technical direction of a company.

Computer network architects can also advance by moving between industries for higher pay. For example, those working for nonprofit organizations or small companies can move to large corporations where pay and benefits are higher. Some computer network architects are self-employed. They work on a contract basis, upgrading a client's network and performing other operations before moving on to the next project. Contract computer network architects can operate internationally and travel the world for clients who need their services.

What Is the Future Outlook for Computer Network Architects?

Computer network architects will remain in demand with firms that are designing and building new IT networks or upgrading and expanding existing networks. However, as more businesses adopt cloud computing, fewer computer network architects will be needed to perform in-house duties. This mixed employment picture means that the demand for computer network architects is not expected to grow as fast as for other IT specialists. The BLS predicts that the computer network architecture profession will grow by 6 percent through 2026, about as fast as average for all jobs. This will result in an additional 10,400 new jobs for computer network architects.

Find Out More

Association for Computing Machinery (ACM)
2 Penn Plaza
New York, NY 10121
website: www.acm.org

The ACM consists of computing educators, researchers, and professionals who promote dialogue, shared resources, and recognition of technical excellence. The association also promotes curriculum recommendations in IT systems, computer science, and software engineering from the middle- and high-school level to the undergraduate, graduate, and doctoral level.

Association of Information Technology Professionals (AITP)
3500 Lacey Rd.
Downers Grove, IL 60515
website: www.aitp.org

The AITP, also known as CompTIA, is a professional organization with 62 local chapters and 286 student chapters at colleges and universities. The association offers webinars, conferences, and job listings to members, and its student program connects students to mentors and provides résumé support and career strategies.

International Association of Software Architects (IASA)
12325 Hymeadow Dr.
Austin, TX 78750
www.iasaglobal.org

The IASA is a community of IT architects focused on training, certification, and continuing education. Members can participate in instructor-led training or self-paced training to pursue an education in computer systems analysis and related IT professions.

Network Professional Association (NPA)
3517 Camino Del Rio S., Ste. 215
San Diego, CA 92108
website: www.npa.org

The NPA is a leading organization for computer network architects and other network professionals. The association offers career advice, certification, and various publications useful to prospective computer network architects.

IT Manager

What Does an IT Manager Do?

One of the highest-paying jobs in the tech industry also has an elongated title that does not exactly roll off the tongue: computer and information systems manager. Little wonder that these highly skilled professionals are most often referred to as information technology managers, or simply IT managers. While the name might be abbreviated, the IT manager's list of duties is not.

IT managers are big-picture thinkers who determine the information technology goals of an organization and coordinate computer-related activities to meet those objectives. The job involves planning and directing the installation and maintenance of computer hardware and software and ensuring that all networks and databases are secure. IT managers use their business acumen to assess the costs and benefits of a project and to negotiate with vendors to get the best prices and levels of service.

Those who work as IT managers regularly interact with others. They meet with executives to ex-

At a Glance

IT Manager

Minimum Educational Requirements
Bachelor's degree

Personal Qualities
Technical knowledge, creative thinking, business acumen, leadership skills

Certification
Network administrator certifications

Working Conditions
Full-time work in an indoor office environment with a high level of social interaction and some stress

Salary
$135,800 median annual salary in 2016

Number of Jobs
367,600 in 2016

Future Job Outlook
12 percent growth through 2026

plain the cost-benefit rationale behind a project. They hire and fire employees, and they work with numerous other IT professionals, including software developers, programmers, network architects, security analysts, and computer systems analysts. Jonathan Dalia is the IT manager for a trucking company called Langer Transport Corporation. He describes his duties on the CompTIA website:

> My job as the IT manager is to configure, setup and maintain all voice, video and data connections at our [four] locations. I check our backups, server hardware and disaster recovery systems on a regular basis. I also fix and troubleshoot issues that arise each day. When I have free time, I look for ways to improve the systems by decreasing costs and [improving] services. I also manage our company's data by writing reports, interacting with our . . . database and writing queries.

Dalia works alone, but at larger companies, the job of IT manager is often divided among several specialists. Chief information officers (CIOs) keep their focus on the future. They analyze their organization's long-term growth plans and work to implement data processing systems and other information technology that will meet those goals. On the Datamation website, IT consultant J. Lance Reese explains why the CIO's job is important:

> The board cares about revenues, profits, and long term viability. Technology is a key component for competitive advantage, opening new markets, and creating an agile infrastructure that can adapt to ever changing competitive sectors and challenges. Any [CIO] talking to the board should be explaining how their technologists are focused on creating business results and developing business solutions, increasing revenues, profits, and growth.

Today's CIOs are focused on cloud computing systems, wearable devices, mobile computing, artificial intelligence, and the Internet of Things in which common appliances and electronics are connecting to the Internet. The job requires CIOs to predict how these digital innovations will affect their companies and how their employers can profit from these changes.

Chief technology officers (CTOs) are IT managers who oversee all technical aspects of an organization. They analyze new technology and determine how it can be deployed to add efficiency or value to their company. CTOs work with CIOs, department heads, executive management, and IT employees to implement a company's strategic technical goals.

Large companies often employ IT directors, or management information systems directors, who are in charge of the organization's IT departments. IT directors determine the business requirements for IT systems and implement policies determined by executives. IT directors hire and fire IT employees and oversee budgets and other financial issues.

IT security managers focus their attention on network and data security. They work with information security analysts to plan security procedures and ensure that they are implemented. When security is breached, IT security managers conduct investigations and report on their findings to company executives.

How Do You Become an IT Manager?

Education

Becoming an IT manager is a long-term goal that requires education, experience, and determination. High school students who hope to work as IT managers one day can take the first steps toward that goal by focusing on math courses, including calculus, statistics, trigonometry, and algebra. Students should take physics and communications, as well as computer science classes.

A bachelor's degree in computer science, information technology, or management information systems (MIS) is a minimum requirement for IT managers. Courses focus on programming, software development, and mathematics. Around one in four organizations require their IT managers to possess a graduate degree such as a master of science in IT management or a master of business administration (MBA). A master's degree can help elevate a job seeker to a better position, as Dave Cox, CEO at LiquidVPN, points out on the Hodges University website: "While the minimum requirement for a computer and information systems manager position may be only a bachelor's degree, a master's degree can surely give you an edge, signaling to hiring managers that you are up-to-date with the latest developments in the world of technology management." Working toward a graduate degree generally takes two years, but some IT managers pursue a master's degree while working their regular jobs, a task that can take longer to complete.

Certification and Licensing

According to a study by the employment website Glassdoor, the position of IT manager is the second-most in-demand job that pays over $100,000. This means that there are a lot of candidates competing for the job. Prospective IT managers will need to seek numerous certifications if they hope to compete with other job candidates in this field.

Cisco, a multinational technology company, offers five levels of certification useful to those moving up the ladder to a position as IT manager. The first level, the Cisco Certified Entry Networking Technician (CCENT), is a starting point for a successful career in networking. It validates that the holder possesses the skills necessary for entry-level network support positions. At the next level, associate certifications can be obtained in important areas of IT management, including network security, network design, cloud computing, and routing and switching. The certificate ladder advances through professional and expert levels. Other vendors also provide certifications for use of their products. Oracle offers certification for MySQL, and Microsoft users can obtain the Certified Solutions Expert accreditation.

Internships

Internships provide an opportunity to observe professional IT managers at work and gain valuable experience managing and troubleshooting problems with computers, software, networks, and other technology. While working as an intern, students can build a human network as well, gaining contacts with those who can provide references and job recommendations after graduation. Some bachelor's degree programs, and most graduate programs, include internships in their curriculums. And many schools have existing relationships with businesses that participate in internship programs.

Skills and Personality

Hernan Santiesteban, founder of the Great Lakes Development Group, describes the importance of skills in IT management on the Hodges University website: "Computer and information systems managers need a wide variety of skills to be successful. Aside from the obvious importance of technical knowledge, oftentimes softer skills can play a more essential role."

Technical knowledge includes a good understanding of circuit boards, processors, chips, computer hardware and software, and other electronics. IT managers rely on analytical and creative skills to troubleshoot networks and equipment and find innovative ways to solve problems. IT managers also rely on logic and reasoning to identify the strengths and weaknesses of the solution they devise to fix a problem.

Business skills are also important. IT managers need to understand economic and accounting principles, banking, and financial data. As Reese explains: "Every IT manager should make business acumen their top priority. Great technologists can be found anywhere; great technologists who focus on business results are rare and valuable."

Soft skills are important to anyone in a management position, and IT managers are expected to be able to smoothly interact with systems analysts, software engineers, project managers, department heads, managers, and vendors. IT managers need to be able to listen to and understand information and ideas presented by others and communicate ideas clearly to team members.

Leadership skills allow an IT manager to motivate teams, plan projects, set company objectives, work with customers, and solve problems. The job requires the IT manager to fairly evaluate employee performance and appoint the best person for each job.

IT managers also recruit personnel, design training programs, instruct individuals and groups, and handle labor relations.

On the Job

Employers

The most desirable jobs for IT managers are at companies that specialize in computer systems design. These firms design and manage computer and information systems and develop custom software for organizations that do not have in-house staff to perform this work. Larger organizations—such as financial and insurance companies, manufacturing firms, and federal, state, and local governments—have in-house IT staff, and all need talented IT managers. The growing health care industry is also increasing its IT use every year and is rapidly creating new posts for IT managers.

Working Conditions

IT managers work full-time, but according to the Bureau of Labor Statistics (BLS), one-third of IT managers worked more than forty hours a week in 2016. Whether an IT manager works forty hours or more, the job can be stressful. Every company relies on its computer and information systems, and failure in one part of the system can cascade throughout the entire network, bringing business to a halt. IT managers are also responsible in part for the financial success of a company. Hiring the wrong employees or investing in overpriced or inadequate equipment can affect a company's bottom line and lead to long-term problems.

Earnings

There is no mystery as to why there is strong competition for IT manager jobs. According to the BLS, the median annual wage for IT managers was $135,800 in 2016. IT managers who worked in the information industry—businesses that collect and sell personal, financial, and other information—earned the highest annual wage at $150,190. Those who worked for computer systems design companies also earned more than the median wage at $143,040. Even those IT managers in the lowest 10 percent earned $82,360 in 2016, more than double the $37,000 annual wage for all jobs.

Opportunities for Advancement

Most IT managers begin their careers at lower-level management positions to gain experience and then advance to higher IT positions. However, some individuals with less experience can find employment as IT managers at companies that are small or just starting up. Typically, after five to ten years of related work experience, managers can advance to the position of IT manager. Within the profession itself, IT managers with exceptional business acumen can advance to CIO or CTO. Those who hope to work as a CIO or CTO usually have more than fifteen years of experience in the IT field. A CIO can move on to become a top company executive.

What Is the Future Outlook for IT Managers?

The BLS predicts job growth for IT managers will grow by 12 percent through 2026, faster than average for all occupations. Demand is expected to come from firms without in-house IT staff that will be hiring computer services companies to move their operations into the cloud. As threats to network security continue to grow, there will be an increased demand for IT managers who specialize in cybersecurity.

Find Out More

Association for Information Systems
PO Box 2712
Atlanta, GA 30301
website: http://aisnet.org

The Association for Information Systems is dedicated to the promotion of excellence in the study of information systems. The association offers educational materials such as webinars and e-books along with training, job placement, and career counseling services.

Association for the Advancement of Artificial Intelligence (AAAI)

2275 E. Bayshore Rd.
Palo Alto, CA 94303
website: https://aaai.org

The AAAI is a scientific society focused on pairing thought and intelligent behavior with computers. Artificial intelligence is spreading into IT applications, and the AAAI offers conferences, workshops, periodicals, and books for prospective IT managers. The society also provides student scholarships, grants, and other honors.

Business Technology Association (BTA)

12411 Wornall Rd.
Kansas City, MO 64145
website: www.bta.org

The BTA serves the technology equipment and systems industry. The association has strong educational offerings, including classroom workshops, webinars and e-workshops, certifications, and scholarships.

Webgrrls International

119 W. Seventy-Second St.
New York, NY 10023
website: www.webgrrls.com

Webgrrls International is dedicated to increasing the number of women in the tech world. The organization connects female computer students with mentorships and internships and features a job bank for women who want to propel their careers forward.

Interview with a
Web Developer

Lauren Cotto has worked as a front-end web developer for the web design company LeaseLabs since 2017. Cotto holds a certificate of completion from the Trilogy Education coding boot camp program hosted at the University of California, San Diego. She answered the following interview questions by e-mail.

Q: Why did you decide to become a web developer?
A: I have been a hobbyist programmer since I was sixteen. During my sophomore year of high school, I took a "webmastering" course. We learned fairly advanced HTML, and built websites for local businesses. After graduation, I went to college and chose to major in electrical engineering, which had me taking some programming courses (Java, C++) as part of my curriculum. For reasons I cannot remember, I decided to go to cosmetology school. I worked as a hairdresser and makeup artist for ten years, and owned a successful salon for three years. As a business owner, I wanted to use Yelp for marketing purposes. Yelp requires any business on its platform to have a website, so I decided I could make one myself. After studying up on modern practices, I built and deployed a site for my business. I enrolled in Trilogy's coding boot camp, started my classes at the beginning of 2017, and have not looked back.

Q: Can you describe your typical workday?
A: A typical workday for me starts with a daily meeting. All the developers in my company will stand around in a circle, and we each talk about what we're working on, if we have any blockers (things interfering with our work, which could be anything from a software bug to hardware complications, and beyond), and if we have any

kudos for our team members. It's a short meeting, usually only lasting fifteen minutes. After that, we go to our desks to work on whatever we have going on for the day. I typically work on mini-projects (small projects that take anywhere from three hours to a couple of days to complete), site builds, or debugging issues from current websites we maintain. I also have two hours of my day set aside for professional development. Currently, I am working on building an app with the JavaScript framework to further my knowledge and that of our team as part of my professional development. I'm usually at work for about eight hours, but it never feels that long!

Q: What do you like most about your job?
A: Every day is like solving a big logic puzzle or going on a treasure hunt. The treasure is a working solution to whatever it is I am doing. I love that I get to use my brain in new ways daily, and am constantly learning new things in order to solve the issues put in front of me. Our company as a whole is very supportive as well, which makes coming to work a joy.

Q: What do you like least about your job?
A: Sometimes, communication between different teams in our office could be better; however, I feel this is normal for many office environments.

Q: What personal qualities do you find most valuable for this type of work?
A: Qualities such as analytical thinking are a given for this type of work. However, soft skills (aka "people skills") are highly underrated and a necessity to be able to work as a developer. Regardless of whether someone works as part of a team or as a freelancer, qualities such as clear, kind, and consistent communication are key to success in this industry. Being able to interact well with others is huge and essential in this industry.

Q: What is the best way to prepare for this type of job?
A: A coding boot camp, like the one I went to, is the best way to prepare for industry trends, but be sure that skills learned are the ones in demand in your local market. Boot camps are structured

and come with excellent support for students so that they can be successful. They are also quick—many are completed anywhere from three to six months. However, boot camps are hard work! They require absolute dedication to the subject matter, and many hours will need to be put in for studying and writing code. Don't look at a boot camp as an easy way out, or a simple route to a new career. They are as much an investment as traditional college.

Q: What other advice do you have for students who might be interested in this career?
A: For anyone out there who thinks they want to be a developer: My best advice to you is to get your feet wet. Go to codecademy. com and learn a language (it's totally free). See if you like it. If you do, then it's time to take the next step and enroll in a boot camp!

Other Jobs in Info Tech

Applications engineer
Applications support analyst
Business analyst
Cloud architect
Cloud consultant
Cloud services developer
Cloud software and network
   engineer
Cloud systems administrator
Computer and information
   research scientist
Computer hardware engineer
Computer programmer
Computer support specialist
Content manager
Data center support specialist
Data quality manager
Digital marketing manager
Director of technology

Electrical and electronics
   engineer
Frameworks specialist
Front-end developer
IT analyst
Java developer
Management information
   systems director
Mobile developer
Network engineer
Social media manager
Software tester
Systems architect
Systems designer
Technical specialist
Technical support engineer
Telecommunications specialist
User interface designer
Web administrator
Web analytics developer

Editor's note: The US Department of Labor's Bureau of Labor Statistics provides information about hundreds of occupations. The agency's *Occupational Outlook Handbook* describes what these jobs entail, the work environment, education and skill requirements, pay, future outlook, and more. The *Occupational Outlook Handbook* may be accessed online at www.bls.gov/ooh.

Index